The Plough and the Stars

Classroom Questions

A SCENE BY SCENE TEACHING GUIDE

Amy Farrell

SCENE BY SCENE
ENNISKERRY, IRELAND

Scene by Scene
11 Millfield, Enniskerry
Wicklow, Ireland.
www.scenebysceneguides.com

The Plough and the Stars Classroom Questions by Amy Farrell. —1st ed.
ISBN 978-1-910949-32-0

Contents

Characters

1. What do you find out about the characters from this list?

2. What does "consumptive" mean?
   What does this tell you about the people in the play?

3. What do you already know about Easter Week 1916?

4. What is a tenement?
   What do you expect life to be like for the tenement residents?

5. What was the Irish Citizen Army?

6. What is a "charwoman"?

7. What was 'The Plough and the Stars'?
   What does this title lead you to expect from the play?

Act One

Summary

This Act takes place in a tenement building, in November 1915.

The characters are introduced. They bicker and squabble throughout the opening Act.

Peter is preparing to attend a Demonstration in Parnell Street at eight o'clock in memory of Irish Patriots.

Mrs Gogan appears as a pass-remarkable woman, with plenty to say about her neighbours.

The Covey and Fluther argue about religion, with Fluther refusing to listen to the Covey's scientific 'rubbish'.

Peter gets annoyed time and again with the Covey, he feels victimised by the way the Covey treats him.

Bessis Burgess is annoyed with Nora, as she complained about Bessie's singing the night before. She grabs Nora and shakes her until Fluther intervenes.

Jack Clitheroe arrives home and comes to his wife's defence, going out after Bessie to warn her to leave his wife alone.

After their tea, the others leave, leaving Nora and Jack to talk together. He says he left the Citizen Army for her, but she doesn't believe him.
A knock is heard at the door, that Nora asks Jack to ignore. It's Captain Brennan, with a message for Jack. Nora is anxious and asks Jack not to open the door, but he does anyway.

The man in uniform has brought Jack a message about a planned attack on Dublin Castle. He tells Jack that he was appointed Commandant a fortnight ago, that a letter was delivered about it.

Jack is angry when he realises that Nora intercepted the letter. She accuses him of thinking only of himself and of forgetting about her when he pursues this cause. Jack grabs her arm, hurting her, before storming out.

Mollser comes in looking for Nora, saying she feels terribly lonely with her mother gone out to the meeting.

Points to Consider

The Plough and the Stars, or Starry Plough was a green and silver flag, the banner of the Irish Citizen Army. The flag shows the constellation known as 'The Plough'. James Connolly, the Irish Republican and socialist leader, co-founded the Irish Citizen Army in 1913. He said a free Ireland would be in control of its own destiny from the plough to the stars, hence the flag's significance. The playwright Sean O'Casey was himself a member of the Irish Citizen Army until 1914.

A lot of information about the Citizen Army and Irish Patriots is mentioned in the opening Act. It is worthwhile to discuss the era and political dimension of the play so that students can better understand the setting and action.

The stage directions give a lot of information about the era of the play. Details such as the picture of Robert Emmet, The Sleeping Venus, The Gleaners and the Angelus are interesting to note. It is worth discussing what these objects tell us about the characters and their world.

Note the antagonism present between the Covey and Peter as it will continue throughout the play. Peter is very easily put out by the other men in the tenement.

The Covey argues with the others about religion. His dismissive view here helps demonstrate his communist outlook . It may be necessary to explain something of the Covey's politics to students, so that they can fully appreciate the exchanges between the Covey and Fluther, who defends religion here.

It is worth noting Mrs Gogan's horror at seeing a painting of a naked woman, something Fluther agrees with her on. There is no question of it being art, it is simply indecent in their view. This outlook may be connected to their traditional religious views.

The close quarters of the characters and the communal nature of their living space is worth noting. This physical closeness may be a factor in the constant petty squabbling and angry outbursts among the residents of the tenement.

Jack tells Nora he left the Citizen Army for her. This is important to draw attention to now, as later he will choose the cause over her.

It is interesting to note that Nora suggests he left the Citizen Army as he wasn't made captain. In her eyes, his decision was entirely about himself, not her at all. It can be useful to ask students to assess this relationship now, and use their views as a reference point later on.

It is interesting to observe how the other characters in this Act view Nora. Her fixation with respectability is interpreted as a sense of superiority over her peers. It is worth considering whether or not their feelings towards her are justified.

It can be rewarding to focus on the characters' gestures in this Act, particularly when they argue, to get a sense of how they express themselves physically. Also, consider whether these exchanges are funny or entertaining and discuss what makes them so.

The knock at the door brings tension to the stage; it is clear that Nora is anxious to avoid the caller. The news he brings moves the action forward, while highlighting conflict between the Clitheroes. Nora accuses Jack of being vain; he grabs her and angrily storms out.

It is worth discussing Nora's actions here, and whether Jack is entitled to his rage and indignance.

It may be necessary to explain what consumption is when Mollser arrives. Also, consider what Mollser's illness suggests about the living conditions in the tenements and the treatment of the poor in Ireland at the time.

The figure or portrait in the window, in the characters list, is generally taken to be Padraig Pearse, one of the leaders of the 1916 Rising. It can be interesting to discuss the significance of this with students.

Questions

1. Describe the Clitheroes' home.

2. Who was Robert Emmet?
   What can you deduce about the household from this picture hanging on the wall?

3. What are 'The Gleaners' and 'The Angelus'?
   What does their presence tell you about the Clitheroes?

4. What is Fluther Good doing as the Act begins?

5. Describe Fluther Good.

6. Describe Peter Flynn.

7. What are your first impressions of Mrs Gogan?

8. What does Mrs Gogan do with Mrs Clitheroe's parcel?
   What does this tell you about her?

9. What comment does she make about Mrs Clitheroe when she opens the parcel?

10. Does Fluther agree with Mrs Gogan's comments about Mrs Clitheroe?

11. What is happening at eight o'clock in Parnell Square?

12. Is Clitheroe involved with the Citizen Army at all?

13. "A couple o' months ago, an' you'd hardly ever see him without his gun." What does this remark of Fluther's tell you about their world?

14. What view does Fluther have of Clitheroe?

15. "You'd want to be careful all th' same." Is Mrs Gogan motivated by kindness when she discusses Fluther's cold?

16. "It always gives meself a kind o' threspassin' joy to feel meself movin' along in a mournin' coach..."
Explain Mrs Gogan's attitude here.

17. Why is Fluther annoyed when Mrs Gogan shows him the 'nightshirt'? What does this tell you about Fluther?

18. Why have the workmen stopped?

19. Fluther remarks, "You can't sneeze but that oul' one wants to know th' why an' th' wherefore..."
What impression does this give you of Mrs Gogan?

20. The Covey says the workers will "march in th' demonstration tonight undher th' Plough an' th' Stars." What do you think this means?

21. What religious attitude does the Covey accuse Fluther of having?

22. "Scientifically speakin', it's all a question of the accidental gatherin' together of mollycewels an' atoms."
What are your first impressions of the Covey?

23. "What about Adam an' Eve?" What do Fluther's comments about religion tell you about religious beliefs during the time the play is set ?

24. How do Fluther's and the Covey's views on religion differ?

25. "You'll be kickin' an yellin' for th' priest yet, me boyo." Is Fluther very religious, in your view?

26. "Oh that's a terrible picture; oh, that's a shockin' picture!" Why does Fluther react like this to the painting? Does this tell you anything about the attitudes of characters in this play?

27. Why does Mrs Gogan leave the room?

28. What makes Peter get annoyed with the Covey?

29. Do Peter and the Covey get on well? Explain your answer.

30. What advice does Fluther give Peter for dealing with the Covey?

31. "He's always thryin' to rouse me." What is your impression of the Covey, based on what you've seen of him so far?

32. Did you find anything about this opening section amusing or entertaining?

33. What is your first impression of Nora Clitheroe?

34. Does Nora manage to quieten the men?
What does this tell you about her?

35. What is Bessie's view of Nora?

36. Why does Bessie attack Nora?

37. What are your first impressions of Jack Clitheroe?

38. What is Nora's role in the household, based on what you have seen so far?

39. How does the Covey provoke Peter?

40. "They're bringin' nice disgrace on that banner now."
Why does the Covey object to the flag of the Plough and the Stars being used in the demonstration?

41. Are the exchanges between the Covey and Peter amusing?
Explain your view.

42. "Are yous all goin' to thry to start to thwart me now?"
What sort of man is Peter, in your view?

43. What reason does Nora give for Jack leaving the Citizen Army? Is she too honest with her husband here?

44. How does Clitheroe singing to Nora contribute to the mood?

45. How does Nora react to the knock at the door?
Does this surprise you or strike you as strange?

46. "How was it word was never sent to me?" Why didn't Jack hear about his appointment as Commandant?

47. How does Jack react to Nora's deception?

48. "You deserve to be hurt."
Does Jack's violence here surprise you?
Is he entitled to feel this way?

49. "I don't care if you never come back!"
Do you believe Nora here? Why is she behaving like this?

50. Describe Jack and Nora's relationship, as you see it.

51. What is the mood like as this Act ends?
Use examples to support your answer.

Act Two

Summary

This Act involves the characters drinking and eagerly listening to talk of rebellion, as they come and go from a public house. The demonstration is taking place, occasionally part of a rousing speech, calling Irishmen to arms, is heard from outside.

The characters are excited by the prospect of rebellion.

Points to Consider

It is worthwhile discussing the historical moment the play is set in, to provide context to the demonstration, speeches and excitement of the public here.

Peter and Fluther, excited by the speeches, argue about Patriotism. Peter mentions his annual pilgrimage to Bodenstown. He is referring to the grave of Wolfe Tone in Bodenstown, Co. Kildare (the poem 'Tone's Grave' by Thomas Davis mourns the failure of the United Irishmen.)

The language of the speaker in the street is worth noting. He speaks of the blood and death of war as something to be welcomed as necessary in Ireland. It can be interesting to discuss why he may feel this way and consider political events taking place at home and in Europe at the time.

Also, it can be interesting to discuss whether students believe this man to have any actual war experience of his own.

Interestingly, these excerpts are attributed to various speeches and writings of Padraig Pearse, the spokesman of the 1916 Rising.

Students tend to enjoy the insults traded by Bessie Burgess and Mrs Gogan in the public house. While amusing, these exchanges exhibit the bitter resentment between the neighbours and show the discontent borne from living at close quarters. It is useful to note these divisions now, for comparison purposes later on, when the women put their differences aside.

Students also tend to react when Mrs Gogan forgets her child and leaves it with Peter (Her consumptive daughter, Mollser, is waiting at home for her).

Both women have had plenty to say about how women should behave and students are quick to note their hypocrisy.

It can be interesting to compare the devotion and commitment of the Irish Volunteers to the average citizens and question whether the sacrifice and bloodshed seems worth it or idealistic and futile.

Questions

1. Describe the scene as Act Two begins.

2. "Nothin' much doin' in your line tonight, Rosie?"
What is Rosie's job? What is your reaction to this?

3. What is the speech being made outside about?

4. "Every nerve in me body was quiverin' to do something desperate!"
What effect has the demonstration had on Peter and Fluther?

5. "The old heart of the earth needed to be warmed with the red wine of the battlefields."
Comment on the imagery and the speechmaker's message here.

6. Do you think the speechmaker has had battle experience? Explain your stance.

7. What does Rosie do when the Covey comes into the bar?

8. What are the Covey's views on freedom?
How would you sum up his political beliefs?

9. Is Rosie interested in the Covey's politics?

10. How does the Covey react to Rosie's advances?

11. How would an audience react to this scene?

12. "I don't want to have any meddlin' with a lassie like you!"
    What makes the Covey reject Rosie's advances, in your view?

13. How has the Covey annoyed Peter this time?

14. What does Mrs Gogan admire about the Foresters' uniform?
    What is your reaction to this?

15. What is significant about Peter's yearly pilgrimage to Bodenstown?

16. "...me own son, dhrenched in water an' soaked in blood, gropin' their way to a shatterin' death, in a shower o' shells!"
    Comment on the imagery in Bessie's speech here.
    How does this contribute to the atmosphere of this Act?

17. "A woman on her own, dhrinkin' with a bevy o' men, is hardly an example to her sex..."
    Does anything about Bessie's words here ring false to you?

18. How does the Covey antagonise Peter while chatting to Bessie?

19. "When war comes to Ireland she must welcome it as she would welcome the Angel of God!"
    Comment on the speaker's sentiment here.

20. Does the Covey share the speaker's views?

21. What do Bessie and Mrs Gogan argue about?

22. In general, do characters appear to get along well with one another in this play?

23. Why does the barman throw the women out?

24. Why does Peter go after Mrs Gogan?
What is your reaction to this?

25. Why does the Covey think that talking to Fluther is a waste of time?

26. How does the Covey infuriate Rosie?
Do you understand her reaction here?

27. "...you're not going to be pass-remarkable to any lady in my company."
Does Fluther's defence of Rosie surprise you here?

28. Why do Fluther and the Covey nearly come to blows?

29. What mood are the Irish Volunteers in when they enter the pub?

30. What is the atmosphere like as the Act ends?

Act Three

Summary

Set during Easter Week 1916, fighting has broken out in Dublin.

Nora is missing as the Act opens. She has been out searching for Jack, something that has been met with scorn by the Volunteers and women she has encountered. They feel every man should be involved in the fighting.

Fluther brings Nora home after her fruitless search for Jack.

Bessie arrives with looted goods. The looting brings a near festive mood to the tenement dwellers, Mrs Gogan and Bessie put their differences aside to go looting together.

Rifle fire rings out and the members of the household rush indoors. Jack appears with Captain Brennan and a wounded Lieutenant Langon.

Nora runs from the house and throws herself on Jack, overjoyed to see him, and he her.

However, at the others' urging, Jack makes it clear that he is going to leave with the Volunteers and admonishes Nora for searching for him. He feels embarrassed by her public displays of emotion.

The Volunteers are keen to leave as Langon is seriously injured. Despite Nora's pleading, Jack chooses the Volunteers over her, pushing her roughly aside.

A drunken Fluther reappears with looted whiskey.

Screams of pain are heard from the house.

Bessie and Mrs Gogan discuss getting a doctor, before Bessie braves the streets in search of one.

Points to Consider

Note that months have passed since the previous Act (set in November 1915), it is now Easter Week 1916.

O'Casey includes references to specific locations involved in the 1916 Rising. It can be worthwhile to explore these references, as students tend to enjoy the 'real life' aspect of the play.

It can be interesting to discuss Nora's determination and dedication in finding her husband. She appears totally committed to him in a way we have not seen before. Some students may question how genuine her emotion is.

Bessie's support of the British can be interesting to discuss. It points towards division and a lack of unity amongst the tenement dwellers. Also, it suggests that the Rising was not supported by everyone.

The characters' attitude towards looting is worth discussing. What is O'Casey suggesting about his characters here? Bessie shows off all she has taken and the others wish they too had been involved, they even suggest looting a pub. Their atttitude is carefree, they do not seem worried about committing theft. They are happy to take advantage of the political situation for their own gain.

Nobody helps the well-to-do woman looking for assistance on her way to Rathmines. Peter claims it's too dangerous, but moments later wants to go "an see th' fun." It can be interesting to discuss whether it is her social class or something else that disinclines the men from helping her.

Bessie and Mrs Gogan have been at odds throughout the play and support opposing sides now that fighting has broken out in Dublin. However, they are united in their shared joy of looting when they take the pram out together. It is worth discussing whether this freshly forged alliance shows a positive sense of neighbourliness or simply self-interest.

It is worthwhile to discuss Nora and Jack's reunion and Jack's subsequent choosing of the Volunteers over his wife, in light of what it suggests about their relationship, and also of Jack's values and beliefs.

The tenement dwellers are looting and drinking, taking advantage of the outbreak of fighting. Are they simply behaving as a modern population might in similar circumstances? It is worth discussing what comment the playwright could be making here. Similarly, the Volunteers' motivation and devotion is also worth discussing.

It can be worthwhile to speculate what is happening with Nora as the Act closes.

Discussion anticipating the story's ending can also be lively at this point.

We won't see Jack alive again. Without giving away this plot development, but bearing it in mind, it is useful to thoroughly discuss Jack's treatment of his wife before beginning the final Act, where we learn of his death.

Questions

1. Describe the scene as the Act begins.

2. How is Mollser's health at this stage?

3. What kept Mrs Gogan awake the previous night?
   How does the imagery she uses affect the mood here?

4. "Oh, here's th' Covey an' oul' Pether hurryin' along. God Almighty, sthrange things is happenin' when them two is pullin' together."
   Does this surprise you?
   Are you inclined to agree with Mrs Gogan?
   How does this affect the audience's anticipation?

5. What state is Dublin city in?

6. Mrs Gogan calls Bessie a "right oul' Orange bitch!"
   What does she mean here?

7. How does Mrs Gogan's dream add to the atmosphere?

8. What condition is Nora in when she arrives?

9. How has she been treated while searching for Jack?
   Why has she been treated this way?

10. Has O'Casey created the impression that the Volunteers are fighting for a worthy cause? Use examples to support your view.

11. What has Nora seen while searching for Jack?
Comment on the imagery here and how it impacts on the play's atmosphere.

12. Why does Nora call the Volunteers cowards?

13. How does Nora view Jack, now that he is gone?

14. "I don't know what I'd have done, only for Fluther."
Are you surprised that Fluther helped Nora here?
How does this add to your impression of his character?

15. Where does Bessie get the new hat, fox fur, umbrellas and biscuits?
Does this surprise you?

16. What reaction do the others have towards her actions here?
What is your response to this?

17. The Covey continues to jibe at Peter, even as Dublin is under heavy artillery fire. What does this tell you about the men and their relationship?
How does it contribute to the scene?

18. "I wonder, would you kind men come some of the way and see me safe?"
The men are reluctant to help this woman. Why, do you think, is this the case?
Are you surprised by their reaction here? Explain your view.

19. "I think I'll go with th' pair of yous an' see th' fun."
What is Peter's attitude to the fighting?
Does this surprise you?

20. What is going on with Bessie and Mrs Gogan and the pram?
Why do they leave together?

21. Peter accuses the Covey of disrespecting the rebels and Volunteers and "revilin' their sacrifice with a riot of lootin' an' roguery!"
Is there truth in what he says?
Is he being genuine or hypocritical here? Explain your view.

22. What has made Bessie and Mrs Gogan see past their differences?
What is your reaction to this?

23. Doe the arrival of Captain Brennan, Lieutenant Langon and Jack Clitheroe change the atmosphere?

24. "Why didn't you fire to kill?"
What do Clitheroe's actions here tell you about his character?
What do Captain Brennan's words reveal about his character?

25. What attitude does Captain Brennan have towards the tenement dwellers?

26. How does Nora react when she sees Jack?

27. How does Jack react when he sees Nora?

28. What does their reunion reveal to you about their relationship?

29. Does this romantic note last for long?
How does Bessie Burgess abruptly change the tone?

30. What condition is Lieutenant Langon in?

31. What reason does Jack give Nora for needing to leave with Brennan and Langon?

32. "I didn't think of th' danger - I could only think of you..."
Is Nora a devoted wife, or is she hysterical and over-emotional here?
Is she a brave character?

33. How does Jack react when he hears Nora has been looking for him?

34. How does Lieutenant Langon's condition add to the scene?

35. What is your response to the way Jack pushes Nora aside to leave with the men?

36. How would you feel in Nora's position?

37. Does Jack's rough treatment of Nora here tell you anything about their relationship?

38. Are you surprised that Bessie brings Nora indoors?

39. What state is Fluther in when he arrives?
How does this contribute to the scene?

40. Why does Bessie leave the house as the Act ends?

41. Are the members of the household supporting one another through this time of crisis?

42. Is this a tense moment as the Act closes? Explain your view.

43. What, do you think, will happen next?

Act Four

Summary

This Act opens in Bessie's upstairs room. A coffin stands nearby, holding Mollser's body and Nora's still-born child. Nora is in a back room, moaning occasionally as the men play cards.

Captain Brennan brings news of Jack's death.

Nora is dishevelled and confused, speaking to a Jack only she can see. The others tell her nothing of Jack's death, due to her fragile state.

Captain Brennan is reluctant to leave, as the British military are everywhere. The men want him gone, but hearing a noise on the floor below, they let him stay.

Corporal Stoddart, a member of the British army, arrives to remove Mollser's body.

Once the body has been removed, the men are taken downstairs. All of the men in the neighbourhood are being rounded up by the British force because of sniper activity in the area.

Nora emerges from her room, intent on laying the table for Jack. She screams for Jack from the window and Bessie struggles with her, trying to move her away from the window to safety.

Two shots ring out and Bessie staggers, hit. She turns on Nora, blaming her for her wounding. Bessie pleads with Nora to fetch help, but Nora fails to do so. Feebly singing a hymn, Bessie passes away.

The British soldiers return to the room, hopeful that they have shot their sniper. They realise that it is Bessie who has been killed. Mrs Gogan leads Nora away, unable to look at Bessie's body.

Corporal Stoddart and Sergeant Tinley have a cup of tea in Bessie's room as the red glare of the sky deepens. Rifle and artillery fire are heard.

The play closes to the sounds of British soldiers singing and the Red Cross calling in the street.

Points to Consider

Mollser's death offstage can catch students off-guard. It may be necessary to consider what her illness suggests about the time the characters are living in. It is also worthwhile to consider how her death impacts on the mood and atmosphere at this point.

Some students may feel tricked or cheated to learn that Nora was pregnant and suffered a stillbirth, while others will feel that this adds to the emotion and sadness of her plight.

News of Jack's death may add to students' sympathy for Nora. It can also lead to an interesting discussion of whether or not he was right to pursue this cause, and what his involvement with the Citizen Army achieved.

Brennan's comment about Jack dying a hero is worth considering. He clearly feels that Jack's death in the name of the cause is worth celebrating. It can be interesting to hear students' views on this.

Captain Brennan's presence when Corporal Stoddart arrives adds tension to the scene. It also raises the interesting discussion of how difficult it can be for the military in circumstances such as these, to identify who is involved in the fighting and who are bystanders.

Bessie's shooting and death is both surprising and shocking. It is worthwhile discussing how she blames Nora for her death, lamenting the care and kindness she has shown her.

Bessie's death is also worth discussing in relation to the way ordinary people's lives are affected by war and armed conflict.

Some students may comment on Nora's helplessness and inaction when Bessie is shot. They may feel frustrated that Nora does so little at such a significant, dramatic moment.

The imagery as the play closes is worth discussing, as is the the presence of the soldiers onstage with Bessie's body.

Questions

1. Describe the scene as the Act opens.

2. What is the playwright communicating to his audience through the setting and props here?

3. What has happened to Mollser?
   What is your reaction to this?
   How does this affect the atmosphere?

4. What condition is Nora in?
   What has happened to her?
   What is your reaction to this?

5. Fluther drinks, stating, "How th' hell does a fella know there'll be any tomorrow?"
   Describe the mood at this point.

6. What news does Captain Brennan bring?
   Comment on the imagery here.

7. "Mrs Clitheroe's grief will be a joy when she realizes that she has had a hero for a husband."
   Comment on Captain Brennan's statement. Is it accurate?
   What does it tell you about his worldview?

8. What does Nora speak of when she appears?
   What does this tell you about her state of mind?
   Do you feel sorry for Nora here?

9. How do Nora's outbursts add to the atmosphere?

10. Why do the men want Captain Brennan to leave?

11. Why has Corporal Stoddart come to the tenement?
    What identifies him as different to the others?

12. "Sure, she's in her element now."
    Is Fluther unkind to suggest that Mrs Gogan will take pleasure in Mollser's death?

13. How do the men react to the Corporal's presence?

14. What is the Corporal's assessment of the fighting?

15. Why does Mrs Gogan thank Fluther?

16. Mrs. Gogan says, "Indeed, it's meself that has well chronicled, Mrs Burgess, all your gentle hurryin's to me little Mollser."
    Relations seem to be very good between the women. Can you explain this turn of events?

17. Why are the British rounding up all of the men in the area?

18. Sergeant Tinley says that the Irish forces are "not playing the goime; why down't they come into the owpen and

foight fair!"
What is your reaction to this?

19. "Jasus, you an' your guns! Leave them down, an' I'd beat th' two o' yous without sweatin'!"
Is Fluther brave here, as the soldiers send the men out into the street?

20. "Jack, Jack, for God's sake, come to me!"
How do you feel as you watch Nora in this final scene?

21. How has Nora and Bessie's relationship changed since we first encountered them?

22. "Merciful God, I'm shot."
Does this development take you by surprise?

23. "I've got this through... through you... through you, you bitch, you!"
Comment on Bessie's rage here.
What does it add to the scene?
What does it reveal about her character?

24. Why doesn't Nora help Bessie here?
What is your response to her inaction here?

25. "They're afther murdherin' th' poor inoffensive woman!"
How true are Mrs Gogan's words here?

26. "Oh Gawd, we've plugged one of the women of the 'ouse."
Is it ironic that Bessie was the victim of a British bullet?

27. What state is Nora in as Mrs Gogan leads her out?

28. Are you surprised that the soldiers have a cup of tea with Bessie's dead body nearly?
    What is O'Casey suggesting by their behaviour?

29. What is significant about the light seen through the window as the play ends?

30. What does Bessie's death suggests about war and violent conflict and the way it affects the lives of ordinary people?

31. Do you like this ending? Explain your view.

32. Who is your favourite character?
    What did you like about them?

33. Who is your least favourite character?
    Why did you dislike them?

34. What impression of Dublin life in 1916 do you gain from this play?

35. What impression of the 1916 Rising do you gather from this play?

36. What message does O'Casey have for his audience in this play?

www.ingramcontent.com/pod-product-compliance
Ingram Content Group UK Ltd.
Pitfield, Milton Keynes, MK11 3LW, UK
UKHW020228250726
13967UKWH00001B/256